I Know You Hear Me, But Are You Listening?

The Doorway to Peace of Mind

By Darryl Bumpass, Sr.

I Know You Hear Me, But Are You Listening?

All rights reserved. No part of this publication may be reproduced, distributed, or transmitted in any form or by any means, including photocopying, recording, or other electronic or mechanical methods, without the prior written permission of the publisher.

I Know You Hear Me, But Are You Listening?

ISBN: 978-0-9898089-4-1
Published by: Darryl Bumpass, CEO
Moneta Menswear Collection (ph)
1-888-286-7158 ext. 2
(F) 732-828-2289
131 w 35th st. New York , Ny 10001

Special Letters to Darryl Bumpass, Sr.

Darryl,

I wanted to savor this piece of writing you did. I enjoyed reading it immensely. It helped me witness the depth of your thought and the passion you have to help others with their journeys of self-discovery. It provokes thought and reflection throughout and the personal references and stories are great. I encourage you to publish and self-publish if a publisher drags its feet on it. Get it out there. Good luck Daryl. Keep me posted.

Dr. Thomas Jordan , PHD

I Know You Hear Me, But Are You Listening?

Dear Mr. Bumpass

I would like to Thank You for your time spent with us students at New Rochelle High School. It was extremely interesting to hear the business that goes hand and hand with the fashion industry. It especially meant a lot to me, listening to someone that is fervent about the industry, even if it comes along with some cantankerous attitudes but you also have the charismatic people that make you even love what your doing even more. That's what you helped me understand. No matter what I want, if I strive to get it I can have it despite what people tell me. I just have to want it enough. Thank You

Sincerely, Imani

To my father:
I never said thank you for bringing me into the world. I would like to say it now. Thank you, Dad! I miss you!

Acknowledgments

Thank you to my God for breathing life into my body and for giving me wisdom and guidance.

Thank you to my family and my foundation: my wife Beverly, daughter Shaquana, and son Darryl Jr.; to my parents Ruffin and Evelyn Bumpass, my sisters Ann and Lisa, and my brothers-in-law Deneil and Eric. To my nephew Lemyers, my niece Danielle, and to the Beasley family, thank you.

Thank you to additional relatives, friends and sources of insight: Paul Anthony Rivers of Sources for Students; Jeffrey Marshall, Brenda Marshall and Jeffrey Marshall Jr.; Rosemond Lucombe, Myron Davis, Clive Anderson, Stan Jones, Les Graham, Darrell Purnell, Tiajuana Robinson, Suzanne Jackson Payne, Denise Jackson Hendrickson, Jade Eleam, Pat Rimes, Curtis

Ingram, Bernard Robinson, Anthony Bullock Rico, Guy Lorrius, Jacqueline Diaz, Celeste Johnson, Ozzie Small, John Pesce, Talent the Comedian, Larry Bird, Magic Johnson, Russell Simmons, Jay-Z, Daymond John, Mercedes Gonzalez of Global Purchasing Companies, Dr. Thomas Jordan, Caren Sgarlato, Kathleen Fasanella of Fashion Incubator, Pastor Deforest B. Soaries Jr., and my best buddy Dutch. A very special thank you to Mr. Eddie Allen; may this be the beginning to many more.

Preface: Who Am I?

My name is Darryl Bumpass. I was born in 1966 and raised in the Bronx and Mount Vernon, New York. I've seen a lot, heard a lot, and been there, wherever "there" might be. I've been kicked out of the U.S. Marines. Locked up in jail for ten months. Suffered with Bell's Palsy. Kicked out of my home in the middle of the night with my wife, daughter and three- month-old son at my side. I have lost money and made money. I have had tremendous success in telecommunications, men's fashion, motivational speaking, consulting, publishing and executive-producing various projects.

Like most of you reading this, I've made good and bad decisions that helped define my life's experience. This book is about mental preparedness and self-mastery. If you're reading it, perhaps you have asked a question about life that led you to this moment. Perhaps you've noticed things taking place right now, for the better or for the worse. Maybe your spirit has been awakened and you're ready for some kind of change. *I Know You Hear Me, But Are You Listening?* is a book that will help you evaluate where you are on your journey and examine the best way to complete the trip. Hopefully, along the way, you will arrive at a destination called "Peace of Mind." Through my story, I hope you can take away helpful guidelines and practical wisdom. I pray that it will ignite an energy within, to let you know that you are greater than you think you are.

Table of Contents

1 Learning to Listen 13

2 Get Out of Your Own Way 23

3 Mr. and Mrs. Distraction 34

4 Rich or Famous? 45

5 Peace of Mind... 54

ABOUT THE AUTHOR 62

The problem in life isn't receiving answers. The problem is identifying your questions.

1

Learning to Listen

Ever had trouble making a decision because you felt like you were being led in different directions? I know I have. My best bet is that pretty much any person who has ever had something serious to think about has been in this position. It might even seem as though you're hearing one inner voice tell you to do something, and another voice telling you to do the opposite.

I know you hear me, but are you listening?

That is the number one question that God and our spirits ask us all the time. Even if you're not a person who believes in a higher power, you've probably experienced those moments when your mind seems to zero in on one particular theme, or repeatedly brings something to your attention.

I know you hear me,
but are you listening?

In my opinion, life can be so easy, but we make it hard on ourselves by not following our intuition. Everybody is a listener; what we choose to listen to comes with our own individual growth. For example, as small kids, we listen to the directions of our parents. Then, as teenagers, we tend to tune in more closely to the opinions of our friends, classmates and other peers. As adults, we get more of a clear sense who we are, our passions, strengths and weaknesses, and we develop a conscience that's based on the values we were taught and the experiences in our lives. This is the stage of adulthood when most of us either build on our intuition or ignore it for a number of reasons. Most of these reasons have to do with the fact that we listen to the wrong things.

In 1993 I decided I wanted to become a fashion designer. I knew nothing about the business or how to get started. I was just a young guy from the Bronx, with no training or degree in the field. I had never even worked in a clothing store. The biggest thing I had in my favor was intuition telling me I could succeed in a big way if I did all the right things, and if I didn't talk myself out of following this dream. I went to the library to research the fashion industry. I poured myself into thousands of magazines and books. Back then, the Internet wasn't widely used, like it is now, so I had to get my information the old-fashioned way. I started out small, printing t-shirts and selling them at different local events.

I Know You Hear Me, But Are You Listening?

DEAR LORD,
I STRETCH MY HANDS TO THEE.
I COME TO YOU FOR YOUR STRENGTH
AND YOUR GUIDANCE.
I KNOW WITH YOU ALL THINGS ARE POSSIBLE.
WHATEVER YOU DO IN THIS SEASON,
PLEASE DON'T DO IT WITHOUT ME.

- Darryl Bumpass Sr

DarrylBumpasssr.com

I Know You Hear Me, But Are You Listening?

I remember walking up and down New York City blocks and speaking to store owners about stocking my product, the shirts, on their shelves. Everyone told me, "No." So after my hopeful start, I began to pack up my dream and haul it in. The shirts that I had proudly displayed to these unimpressed retailers would go back into the same boxes that I'd carried them in. As I sat in my car one day after all the rejections, I heard Dream Snatchers whispering in my ear: "You can't do it. You know nothing about fashion. You know nothing about fabrics or palettes. All you're doing is putting your labels on something that looked just as good without it."

I could have listened to that nonsense, but instead I listened to my intuition and my spirit. After all the "no's" I had heard on that long day, and so many other days, I decided to try one more store on Gramatan Avenue in Mount Vernon. To my surprise, the owner checked out my original designs and said five words I'll never forget: "We'll take everything you have."

What a rush!

Before I knew it, my t-shirts were in multiple stores, being seen on TV and worn by celebrities. This was my confirmation of the difference between *hearing* and *listening*. What I heard that day, before I drove out to Mount Vernon, was the voice of doubt. Discouragement. Disbelief. Who did I think I was to believe I could jump out into a huge city, in a big competitive field, and make my mark when I didn't even have any experience? I heard all sorts of questions like that in my own mind, but what I listened to was the other voice. It said, *"You can do it. Don't give up."* That one last effort – after I sat in my car thinking about surrendering it all to the Dream Snatchers – is what turned everything around.

The problem in life isn't finding answers. The problem is identifying your questions. Mine were: *Are you ready to quit? Have you given this your all?* Once you get the questions right, the answers will always come. You might feel some intuition about what should happen next. Listen to it! The next step is that you be watchful and alert. Sooner or later, what seem like "coincidences" will move you in the direction indicated by your intuition. This is The Celestine Prophecy.

Just as I was writing this, my phone rang and my aunt told me that my uncle had passed away. As tears ran down my face and onto the page, I thought of how he introduced me to entrepreneurship when he hired me to work for his landscaping business. His death was six years to the date that I lost my father to cancer. I thought of how that shook my foundation. These personal losses helped remind me that I'm not invincible and that we can never take time for granted. The deaths of others should help us remember to ask ourselves questions:

    Why am I here?

    What is my blueprint? What are my goals?

    How can I make a difference in the world and, also, in other people's lives?

    Then we have to watch and wait for the answers. Isn't it funny how

many of us get down on our knees to pray, and

then we just get right up, instead of staying there for a minute to listen? They say patience is a virtue. I know I have to be patient with myself, to recognize the differences between what I'm hearing about my life's directions and what I'm actually listening to – what I'm processing. I have to be patient enough to learn and understand the best ways to pursue my dreams and visions. I have to remember, whenever I'm confused, doubtful, or discouraged that, before I can find the answers, I have to ask myself: What are my questions?

Have you asked yourself any questions today?

I Know You Hear Me, But Are You Listening?

Fear is a disease that can contain you

2

Get Out of Your Own Way

In 2004, I began my transition from a man to a *full-grown* man. I realized that my inner maturity had to match my physical maturity. Based on the success of my t-shirt sales, I established my clothing company Strictly Bump One. Now it was time to challenge myself. In order to grow my brand, I knew I couldn't limit the clothing line to t-shirts. But finding my way to the next level presented new obstacles. Where would I get the resources? Courage and determination got me in the doors of retail shops around New York. I had scored a victory, but my journey was far from complete.

Have you ever started down a road, then reached an intersection and not known where you should turn? We do that a lot in life, and not just while driving or walking. We cross the first hurdle or two, but can't figure out how to get to the finish line. At times like this, we have to get out of our own way. What I mean by that is, too often, we don't know what the next move should be, so we stand still. Think about that goal to start a new business or program you've had in mind, but you've been putting off because you just didn't know how to do it. The longer you put it off, the more you're at risk of falling into one of the traps of the Dream Snatchers. If you've ever made any of the following statements, you might have already slipped and fallen into a "dream pit":

"I work a nine-to-five. I just don't have time to start a business." "I don't know anything about running a company."

"It's too risky."

"I'm afraid of failing."

"I'm too_____(fill in the blank with "old," "young," "broke," "uneducated," etc.).

Sound familiar? If so, pull yourself out of the dream pit. The Dream Snatchers want you to stay there – but they're not the ones standing in your way. Imagine a person who is your identical twin, from head to toe; same height, same weight, same body structure. If you're standing still, instead of making a move – any move – toward your goal, it's the same as having this identical twin block your path, no matter which way you go: If it's right, left, or side to side, your body double stays in front of you.

Get out of your own way!

Start small. Maybe your goal is to travel across the country, but you've never even left your house. Your first challenge should be crossing the street. Cross the street every day for a week until you get used to it. Look back at your house every time and see how far you've gone. Spend the next week walking around the block; and the week after that riding through the city on a bus or in a cab. You get the idea. Lack of time, lack of confidence, or lack of ability can never be excuses for standing still.

I Know You Hear Me, But Are You Listening?

"If you're above ground, you're winning.
If you're breathing, you're winning."
Darryl Bumpass Sr

Expanding my company beyond t-shirts required that I get help. I knew I couldn't do it alone. I began to seek out people who could help me become a better clothing brand and a better person. I wanted people around me who could help me grow, professionally, mentally, and spiritually. You always want to surround yourself with people who have great insight in their respective fields, but not just to help you in business. Maybe you're a factory worker who wants to become a motivational speaker; or maybe you're a single mom who wants to write her first novel. There isn't always a degree or training program that prepares you for everything you need to know. You will constantly learn and grow from the insights and seeds planted in you by other successful, positive mentors.

So I met the very smart and beautiful Mercedes Gonzalez of Global Purchasing Companies. She helped me understand what I needed, in order to launch Moneta Menswear, and she explained to me what business avenues I should pursue. Before I knew it, I was in Bogota and Medellin, Colombia building relationships with clothing factories. A few months later, I was on a twenty-two-hour flight to Addis Ababa,

Ethiopia making more connections. I even had breakfast with the United States ambassador to Ethiopia. If I had stood in my own way because I didn't know what to do next, I might never have looked outside New York. But just by asking someone for help, I left my "house" and crossed the street to significant growth.

An important thing to do, now and then, is challenging ourselves. Living in the Bronx, I heard a lot of Spanish, but I didn't know how to speak it. I had no idea, just a few months before I started traveling and after I had decided to take Spanish lessons, that I would be using it so soon, speaking to business contacts like those in Lima, Peru, who started producing some of my new clothing products. Sometimes, just forcing ourselves to try a new experience or take up a hobby opens doors that help lead us to success. Albert Einstein said, "A person starts to live when he can live outside himself." Force yourself to grow!

I always say to myself, "This time next year, I will be...," or "This time next year I will have done..." It's a way to make sure that I always set new goals. Try writing down your own. Remember, just like in court, if it's not on paper it doesn't matter. You might not reach the goals on your list in the same order that you wrote them, but trust me, they will happen if you get out of your own way. They will happen if you make the effort.

Through a combination of experiences, my mental growth has become immeasurable. I'm able to say hello and goodbye to fear. Fear is a disease that can contain you. Fear will make you believe you can't become the person you're trying to become; the person God has planned for you to be. Fear is a liar and a de-motivator. Fear will keep you stuck in the past and keep you believing you can't overcome your mistakes. Gospel artist Kirk Franklin has a great song called "Hello Fear." I implore you to give it a listen. Your season to win starts now. Don't be afraid. Go get it!

I'm now aware of the bad energy that tries to enter my life.

3

Mr. and Mrs. Distraction

As I write these words, I can feel my spirit and heart starting to warm. As I grow, so does my relationship with God. I know now that I'm not lucky, but blessed. Blessed to be alive! If you're above ground, you're winning. You're winning even when you think you're losing – because you still have opportunities to go after the win! When the suggestion to write this book was whispered to me I must admit it was truly a blessing to have Mr. Paul Anthony Rivers in my life. He gave me the direction on how to publish this book. We don't have to know everything or have every piece of the puzzle in place before we start chasing a dream. Sometimes others have been put in our lives to do work we can't do on our own, or to pass along the encouragement we need at key moments. I understand that chasing goals can be hard, but nothing worthwhile comes without hard work. In the words of actress Mae West, "I never said it would be easy. I only said it would be worth it."

So don't expect that you won't ever run into traffic jams or detours on your journey. Let me introduce you to Mr. & Mrs. Distraction. We all know of someone or something that competes for our attention, no matter how many times we say to ourselves, "Stay focused." True focus is a level that only a few people can truly achieve, and it comes with what sometimes adds up to years of practice. I'm not talking about the kind of focus that means you're able to concentrate on a test for forty-five minutes; I mean being able to keep a goal in sight for six months, a year, or as long as it takes for you to succeed. I know Mr. Distraction well. At times, he even seems like my best friend. He's the guy that can make me think I'm missing something on TV. He can make me believe I don't need to work out this week. "A few days off won't make a difference," is the kind of thing he might say.

Mr. Distraction can help you come up with excuses for not pursuing your dreams. He'll tell you your day job is so great that it would be silly for you to step outside your comfort zone. "Life is good here. What are you complaining about?" he'll ask. Or Mrs. Distraction might use the fear factor, telling you that if you go after a dream, you'll be neglecting your family in the process.

"You don't have time to work forty hours and then spend extra time taking a real estate course," she'd say. The truth of the matter is that we should all be creating financial freedom for ourselves and our families, so we don't have to depend on a job.

" Surround yourself with success, not with Mr. & Mrs. Distraction."

-Darryl Bumpass Sr

Mr. or Mrs. Distraction will tell you to forget your discipline: "Go and buy anything you want. You can put the money back later." But you can never put back what you already spent. You can never put back time or money! You can only add to money. Once it's spent, you can replace the amount that you used, but you'll never have as much as you would have if you didn't spend it in the first place.

I recall being invited to Nigeria for a speaking engagement. I was so excited when I got the email. I started putting my Power Points together and packing my clothes. Even in all my eagerness, I got tag-teamed by Mr. & Mrs. Distraction. They kept pointing out reasons why I shouldn't go: "It might not be safe over there. Stay here and work on your spring/summer collection." Now, there's always an argument to be made against neglecting work, and my spring/summer collection was important to me. But I might not have gotten another opportunity to speak in Africa. I was planning to go. Then Hurricane Sandy hit New York in 2012. That's what you call a distraction! I couldn't make my trip because the whole city shut down. Sandy made me think about Hurricane Katrina and how it devastated New Orleans and other parts of the South. Back then I was still in the early stages of pursuing my dream when I felt the call to join the volunteers and help out. Guess who showed up to tell me I should stay home and focus on building my business – that same old couple, Mr. & Mrs. "D." I heard them, but unlike the advice in the first chapter, I wasn't listening! I had to tune them out, in order to go after a goal.

Maybe you're asking, "But wasn't the goal

to build a career in men's fashion?" My answer is yes, that was the main goal and my big dream. But we can't let ourselves get confused between neglecting goals and taking those rare opportunities to advance or expand our life's experience. Sometimes there's such a thing as being too focused, but this is another trick of Mr. & Mrs. Distraction. We should never have tunnel vision to the point that we ignore things just because they don't fit our agenda, when these things could benefit ourselves or others. Selfishness limits success. Had I listened to Mr. & Mrs. Distraction, I wouldn't have had the life-changing experiences of working in Louisiana, Mississippi and Florida to help people who had lost everything they had. I'm richer as a person for having volunteered my time and energy. New experiences help prepare us for new goals.

Just remember that no person or thing should be allowed to distract you from doing what you consider important. You are the beginning and the end of your dream.

Here are ten of the most common things that distract us from long-term and short-term goals:

1. Looking for others to make us happy

2. Food

3. Money

4. Being too eager to please others

5. Giving in to pressure

6. Not meditating

7. Not working out

8. TV

9. Fear

10. Neglecting our own needs

Number ten is so important. I have one day a week that I like to call D.M.D. ("Do Me Day"). Your "Do Me Day" can consist of anything you want. If you would like to catch up on some reading, go ahead. If you want to spend it listening to music, you can. If you want to meditate and then go jump on a roller coaster, you should do that; all because it's D.M.D. You don't want to get to the point of feeling like chasing your dream means not having fun or never being able to relax. Besides giving you a break, "Do Me Day" helps you become more alert to the distractions around you. It's easier to process more of what you see and hear, whether good or bad, during "down" time. I'm now aware of the bad energy that tries to enter my life because D.M.D. helped me to step away from it. I'm able to see things from a little more distance, and that helps me to decide when I need to stay on a particular course or change my direction, whether personally or professionally.

Take breaks to "do you" and you'll always feel refreshed when it's time to get back to the business of chasing dreams.

Discipline is not a bad word. Discipline equals success.

4

Rich or Famous?

"Do you want to be rich or famous?"

Mercedes Gonzalez, of Global Purchasing Companies, asked that question at her seminars. I was always interested in hearing the responses people gave. I don't think there's any right or wrong answer, because the answer might lie in what you want out of life itself. Not everybody wants to be "rich," but most of us want to be financially comfortable. Not everybody wants to be famous, because many of us value our privacy. If you're looking for fame these days, you might not need to do much more than create a social media page and generate a couple of "followers." If you want to become rich, you should ask yourself, "Do I need short money, or generational wealth?" Generational wealth takes time. A plan needs to be set for building and maintaining income for the next five, ten, twenty, even thirty years. The span that it takes for us to continue developing substantial amounts of money might mean the difference between being rich, temporarily, and being comfortable well into the future.

But achieving any goal takes self-control. Emotional decision-making has to be replaced with business decision-making. If it doesn't make dollars, it doesn't make sense. Even when it's not a money issue that you're addressing, put a value on it: How does it impact your ability to reach your goal? Does it add to your ability to move ahead, or does it take away from that ability? Does it create a positive result, or does it waste time and energy? And what are you willing to sacrifice? Put a value on everything that has the potential to push you forward or pull you back. Can you sacrifice some of the things you want to do, for the things you need to do?

In the same way that athletes train their bodies for big competitions, training your mind takes time. The mind is where discipline begins. So if your mind and spirit are in balance, why shouldn't you want your bank statement to reflect a great balance, too? When I wanted to make some kind of sense out of my life I began putting all my assets and liabilities on paper. This was the moment when I realized I was letting my money get away from me. I was paying everyone else – I mean everyone else – and not paying myself. I was paying other companies that did business with me, and not adding money into my own resources, like the cost of advertising, for example. I was paying anyone who had a sob story about how broke he was. I emphasize that I was paying for the sob story because it usually came in the form of a loan request, but it's only a loan when somebody pays it back, right? If your loan isn't repaid, it means you bought yourself a sob story.

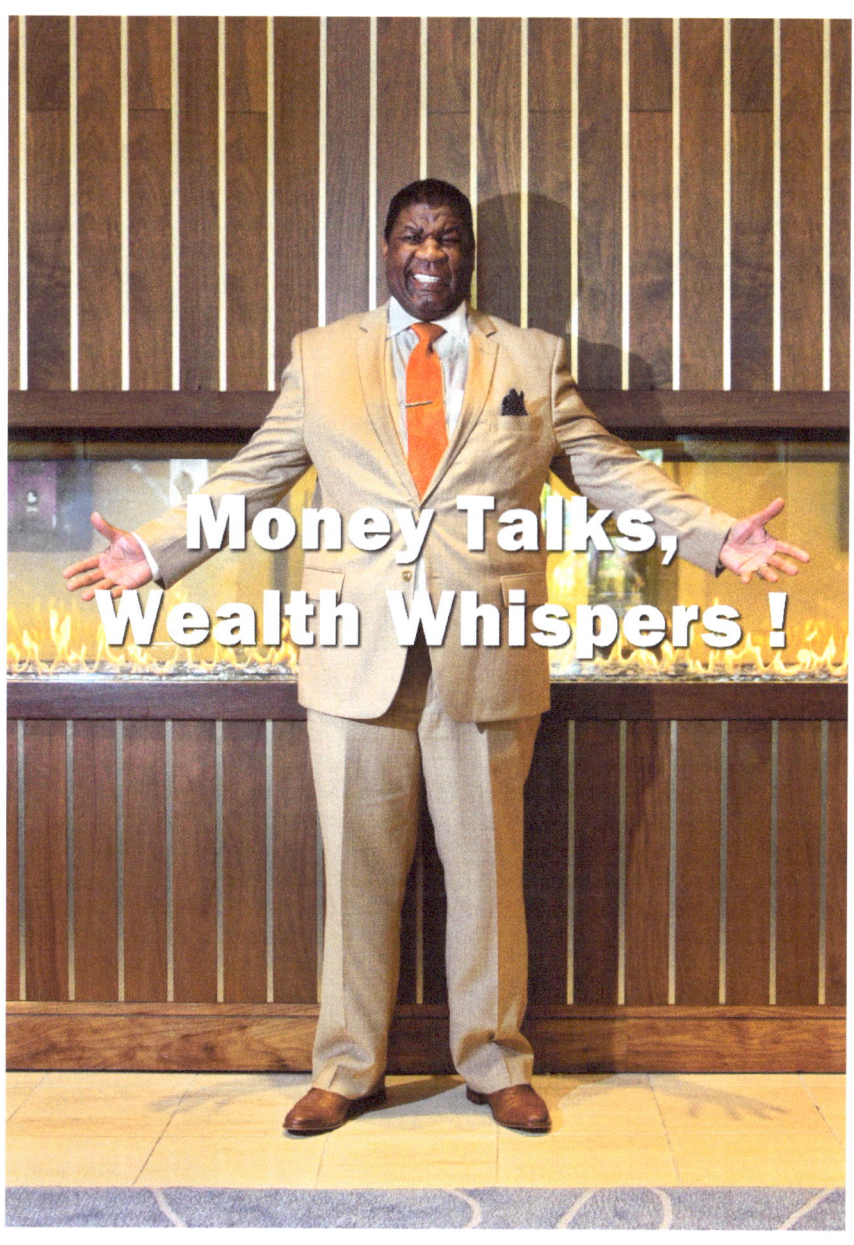

I decided that I had to start paying myself. And again, it wasn't just in terms of money. I had to include more of the things in my life that had value and eliminate things that lacked it. Just like when you're sitting at the computer, hit the "delete" button on anything or anyone that's not helping you grow. I don't mean to say that you can't be kind to others, too, but don't go so far out of your way to build up another person, financially or otherwise, that you put yourself at a disadvantage. Limit your access to people, places and things that don't benefit your mind, your spirit or your bottom line.

I had to make financial adjustments and mature decisions to keep myself on the right track. I closed accounts that weren't showing me great returns. I explored investments that would help me make money, even while I slept. I sat down with a financial planner, Caren Sgarlato. She became a windshield wiper to help me see my financial future more clearly. Whatever financial freedoms I hadn't experienced were self-imposed. In the same ways that we're responsible for our own success, we're responsible for making ourselves as secure as possible while pursuing it. At the same time, if you're confident and sure of your gifts and skills, money will always find you.

The key to it all still points back to discipline. If discipline is a problem area for you, start holding yourself accountable. One simple way to start is by writing what I call a "promise letter" to yourself. Read it until you believe it, and treat it as a real set of promises that you're responsible for keeping. Yours should be based on your own dreams, morals and beliefs, but here's the first one that I wrote:

> I promise everyday to give 100% dedication to my vision.
> I promise, if I slip, trip, stagger or fall, I will get right back up. I promise to be a magnet for my own growth.
> I promise to enjoy the process of finding God's blueprint for my life. I promise to build other people up.
> I promise to LOVE myself first.
> **I PROMISE TO KEEP THESE PROMISES!**

Peace of mind isn't something you can order at a take-out spot. There's no 1-800 number for it.

5

Peace of Mind

I've saved my best advice for last. I could speak about this subject all day, every day, because it's a topic that is very dear to my heart. The topic is peace. Peace of mind isn't something you can order at a take-out spot. There's no 1-800 number for it. And it's not something you can barter for. Peace of mind is something that you have to court. I compare courting peace of mind to dating someone and saying to yourself, "This is the one!" You have to treat this idea of achieving inner peace like it's the person of your dreams; like you'll do almost anything to have it in your life, and almost anything to keep it, once it's received.

To have the best for yourself, goal-wise, peace of mind is required, but to have peace of mind, you also have to fall in love with you. There's no such thing as gaining peace when you think that any car, house, trip or relationship connection will bring it to you. It starts with God and with you. In the last chapter, I described money as a means of building security and comfort for yourself and for your family – which makes it easier for you to focus on your dream – but don't let material things define the dream itself. Material things are just by-products of the goals you have accomplished. Material things come and go. If the only dream you ever had for yourself was to buy a new car and it got totaled in an accident, what does that say about your dream? No, the dream has to start and end with your development as a person – career-wise, experience-wise, and education- wise. Peace of mind opens the door to all these things.

So what opens the
door to peace of
mind? Truth.

To receive truth, we must be willing to face frightening realities about ourselves that rebel against it, and this takes courage. Accepting truth into our lives means rolling up our sleeves and beginning the arduous task of changing what's wrong in our thoughts, attitudes, and behavior, and this takes diligence. Through our own process of receiving truth, we resist the tendency to become critical and condemn others who are still in the truth- seeking process. This takes humility. While there are a lot of components to the long journey toward gaining and maintaining peace of mind, it helps us fight frustration, discouragement and other elements that interfere with reaching goals. The biggest goal I've set for myself is maintaining peace of mind. It's a gift, but not one that comes without adversity. When adversity threatens your peace of mind, treat it like a knife-sharpener that helps you develop your coping and life skills. At the same time, don't get so used to adversity that you give in to it. Peace of mind can be right outside the door of adversity, but when it knocks, we have to let it in. When stress, drama, gossip and sickness knock, we are so quick to open the door. We don't just open it, we say, "Welcome."

-Darryl Bumpass Sr-

Sometimes I've been awake at 3 a.m. when I needed to get up at 5 a.m. In order to grab some peace of mind I needed to write down my thoughts, like in a journal. I find this very therapeutic. It goes back to the courtship process and courting peace of mind the way you court someone you love. I know how it feels to love someone with every fiber in your body and not have that same love returned. Your peace of mind can grow from how you love others, but also from loving yourself. Peace and happiness should not depend on how someone else makes you feel. What someone else does for you, emotionally, financially and materially can only lead to a false sense of security if you connect these things with inner happiness. The object is to become more independent. Dependency equals slavery!

Love yourself enough that you don't let anyone or anything else own real estate in your mind. In the meanwhile, give love to others freely, without expectation or conditions. Since love and peace go hand in hand, love will also attract peace of mind. Here's my thought about spreading love:

I Know You Hear Me, But Are You Listening?

I Love You

I Love You more than you will ever know.

I Love You even when you don't say a word.

I Love You for knowing when to say the right words. I Love You for the times you sacrificed your happiness for mine. If there's ever a time that you doubt my love, read this again.

I Love You. I Love You. I Love You.

So when I'm no longer here, remember me for my biggest achievement: How I loved you.

"I see you,
I thank you
and
I appreciate you."

- Darryl Bumpass Sr

I know you hear me, but are you listening?

ABOUT THE AUTHOR

Darryl Bumpass is founder of Moneta Menswear and Strictly Bump One Clothing. Based in New York and New Jersey, Darryl is an entrepreneur and self-taught fashion expert. His Strictly Bump One design has been worn by the BET cable network's former "106 & Park" host Terrence Jay and multiple celebrities. In addition to his fashion career, Darryl is an executive producer of concerts, a motivational speaker and author. He is also a dedicated philanthropist who participates in clothing drives for the homeless, cancer cure initiatives, and events for underprivileged youth.

www.ingramcontent.com/pod-product-compliance
Lightning Source LLC
Chambersburg PA
CBHW040355190426
43201CB00037B/12